LIFE WORKS!

FEELING GREAT

HOW TO STAY POSITIVE

by Sloane Hughes

BEARPORT
PUBLISHING

Minneapolis, Minnesota

Credits: 6, © weily/Shutterstock; 7, © wavebreakmedia/Shutterstock; 9, © FatCamera/iStock; 12, © Sergey Novikov/Shutterstock; 13, © Yuliya Evstratenko/Shutterstock, © tarubumi/Shutterstock; 16, © ANURAK PONGPATIMET/Shutterstock, © Krakenimages/Shutterstock; 20, © Deepak Sethi/iStock; 22, © Roman Samborskyi/Shutterstock; 23, © annebaek/iStock.

Bearport Publishing Company Product Development Team
President: Jen Jenson; Director of Product Development: Spencer Brinker; Managing Editor: Allison Juda; Associate Editor: Naomi Reich; Senior Designer: Colin O'Dea; Associate Designer: Elena Klinkner; Associate Designer: Kayla Eggert; Product Development Specialist: Anita Stasson

Library of Congress Cataloging-in-Publication Data is available at www.loc.gov or upon request from the publisher.

ISBN: 979-8-88509-965-3 (hardcover)
ISBN: 979-8-88822-142-6 (paperback)
ISBN: 979-8-88822-285-0 (ebook)

For more information, write to Bearport Publishing, 5357 Penn Avenue South, Minneapolis, MN 55419.

CONTENTS

FEELING GREAT!

We have big smiles and are standing tall. How are we feeling? Great! Thinking good thoughts about just one thing can make everything a little better.

It makes it easier to face **challenges**. We can be good friends and get more things done. How are you thinking?

ADD A POSITIVE

When we are **positive**, we think about good things. Being **negative** means **focusing** on the not-so-great. Like in math, being positive can add up.

Me + Positive thinking =
A GREAT DAY!

I love being a monster!

How we think is important. More positive thinking means we feel better.

When's the last time you felt positive about something? Did it add anything to your day?

CAN'T TO CAN

When something happens that is big and hard, it can be tough to think positive thoughts. Everyone faces challenges sometimes. That's okay. This helps us grow.

But when we face these things with negative thoughts, they are much harder. What happens when we turn *can't* into *can*? That's a positive change!

TURN IT AROUND

Let's try changing our thinking.

TRY IT:

CAN DO

1. Think of something that is hard but that you are working on.

2. Take a piece of paper, and write that you can't do the thing.

3. Now, cross out "can't."

4. Change the sentence to a positive. "I can do it!"

WHAT WE CONTROL

We don't have control over everything. But we can always work to bring something positive into our day!

Try to focus on the positive steps we can take when something doesn't go as planned.

When something negative happens, we can treat ourselves with kindness and care. This helps us feel positive again.

EVERYDAY INTO ART

Practice taking what you have and making it positively beautiful.

TRY IT:

STICK ART

1. Gather a handful of sticks, rocks, or everyday objects.

2. Move these things around to make a pretty picture.

3. Try again. How else can you take these everyday objects and make them beautiful?

SOLUTIONS

Many problems big and small can be solved. When we make positive changes, we can find **solutions**.

Choosing to do something for others often helps us feel great!

DONATIONS

Even small things can help make the world a more positive place!

17

TAKING ACTION

Notice how often you find solutions to turn problems positive.

TRY IT:

BRACELET GAME

1. Put a bracelet or rubber band on your wrist.

2. Notice when you have a problem.

3. Every time you come up with a solution, switch the bracelet to your other wrist.

4. How many times can you switch it in a day? In a week?

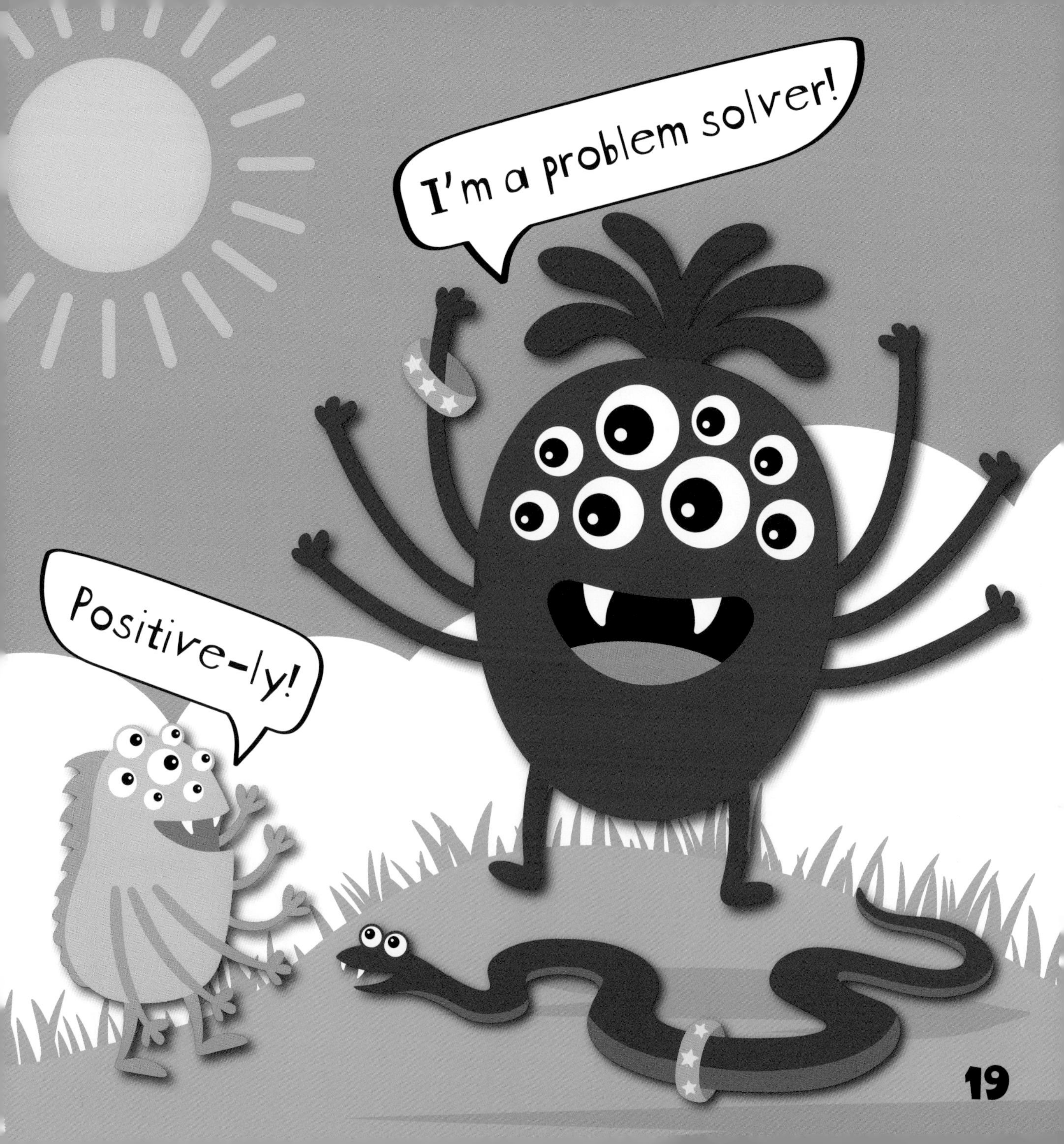
I'm a problem solver!
Positive-ly!

GRATEFUL

Another way to feel amazing is to think about all we have. We feel **grateful** when we notice the good things already in our lives.

Who or what are you grateful for? Make a list!

We can think about all the things that make us happy. Favorite toys may make us smile. And our best friends are sure to make us feel positive.

POSITIVELY GREAT

We can choose to be positive. That thinking helps us feel great! Then, everything is better. When we feel great, there is no telling what we can do.

23

GLOSSARY

challenges difficult things to do

focusing giving your full attention to something

grateful feeling thankful for something you have or something that has been done

negative something that takes away or makes things harder

positive something that adds or makes things better

solutions answers to problems

INDEX